"Anteater Analogy"

Written and Illustrated by: M.C. McNellis

Copyright © 2014

For Nadia, my first fan.

The anteater is a mammal that inhabits a large portion of South America and part of Mexico. There are four species of anteater in the suborder Vermilingua, meaning "worm tongue." The smallest is about the size of a squirrel; the largest is about the size of golden retriever. All anteaters are capable of walking on the ground, climbing trees, and digging.

SOUTH AMERICA

Silky Anteater

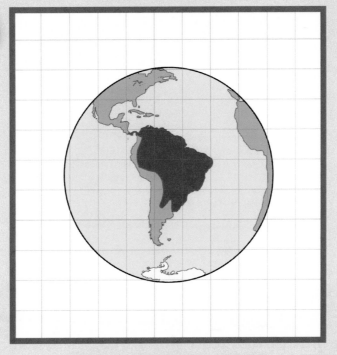

THE ANTEATER ZONE

Giant Anteater

Southern Tamandua

Northern Tamandua

The anteater has a diverse family tree. Its relatives include other extreme looking mammals such as the pink fairy armadillo, the pangolin, and the sloth.

The anteater species evolved to have a very specialized diet. Anteaters are insectivores and will eat spiders, bees, beetles, worms, grubs, larvae, and occasionally fruit.

Despite the name, the anteater prefers termites as its primary food source.

 EATER
EXHIBIT THIS
WEEK AT
THE ZOO!

Its long snout has no teeth, limited jaw movement, and proportionally the longest tongue of any mammal. This snout doubles as a snorkel for the anteater when it enjoys a swim.

The anteater's two-foot long tongue is covered in tiny hooks and sticky saliva that makes this appendage function like fly paper. Since it cannot chew, the insects are mashed against a hard palate in the back of the anteater's mouth.

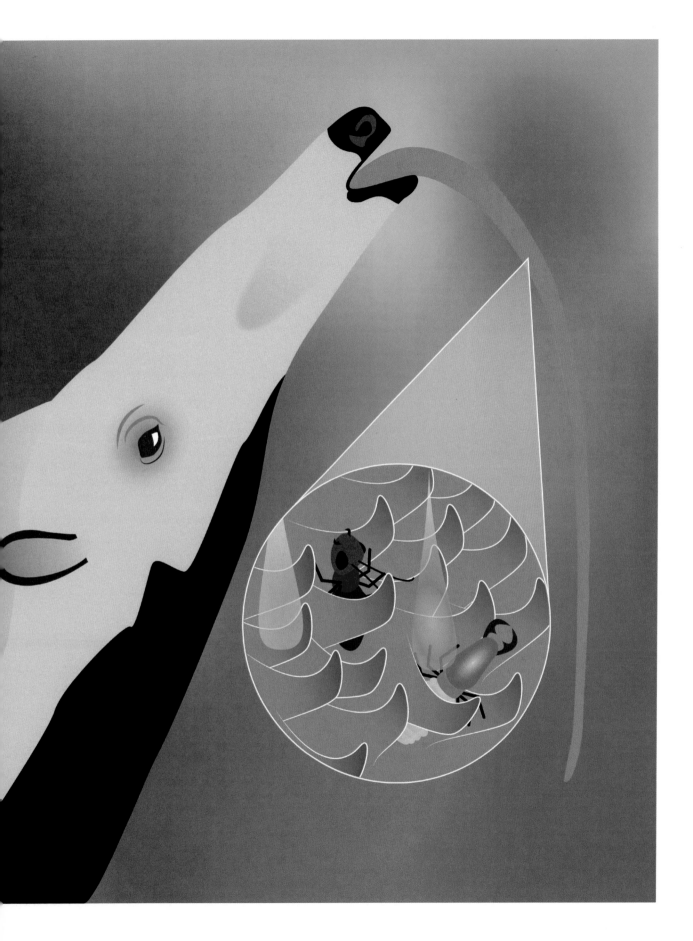

All anteaters are cool. They have a very low body temperature of about 91 degrees Fahrenheit. This is a few degrees lower than most mammals, which is typically between 97-100 degrees Fahrenheit.

The anteater has very poor eyesight and relies on its dog like nose to find food.

Insects are a great source of nutrition for the anteater. Termites and ants contain more protein than beans, meat, and nuts. A giant anteater consumes up to thirty-five thousand insects in a single day.

GIANT'S CHOICE

CONTAINS: 30,000 TERMITES
GREAT SOURCE OF PROTEIN

CANT SNUFFLE ENOUGH!

The anteater must use a bit of strategy when foraging. It feeds from many different termite and ant mounds throughout the day, visiting each for only about a minute at a time before the residents have a chance to attack.

With a tongue flicking rate of one hundred sixty times per minute and an abundance of insects available, the anteater is able to "hoover" up plenty of insects to satisfy its appetite.

The anteater lumbers from mound to mound walking on its knuckles, like a gorilla. Walking this way keeps the claws on the front feet sharp for opening insect nests.

An anteater sleeps up to fifteen hours a day on the ground in secluded areas of the forest using its tail like a blanket.

Even though it has small ears, the anteater is a very light sleeper and can wake at a moments notice to escape or defend against potential danger.

Its large size makes the giant anteater vulnerable when sleeping or foraging. Although it would rather run than do battle, an anteater will fight to protect itself against ferocious predators such as pumas and jaguars. When threatened it will stand up on its hind legs, using its tail for balance, and make slashing motions with its sharp claws.

The giant anteater's claws are among the largest of any mammal, rivaling those of even large bears.

Each anteater independently claims a territory up to one and a half square miles by leaving its scent around the area. It sprays trees and bushes to let other anteaters know this spot is taken.

FOR ALL YOUR TERRITORIAL NEEDS

BOTTLE YOUR
PERSONAL SCENT
TODAY!

The solitary life of an anteater is interrupted during mating season…

…and when a mother gives birth. The pup rides on her back where it is camouflaged from predators. The stripes of the pup align with the mother's in a way that makes the pup almost disappear into her coat. The two typically stay together for nine to ten months or until the pup is able to be independent from the mother and claim a territory of its own.

Anteaters are generally quiet but will communicate with each other by snorting, hissing, and sniffing.

Although it has a bizarre appearance and unique adaptations, the anteater typically leads quite an uneventful life of snuffling out food and occasionally quarreling with neighbors or predators.

To learn more about anteaters visit your local library!

Made in the USA
Monee, IL
18 March 2020